Beeus Finds Her Way Home. Copyright © 2022. Author Sue Spencer Cannon. All rights reserved. No part of this book may be reproduced or used in any manner without written permission except for the use of quotations in a book review.

You can contact the author at suescannon@gmail.com

For all of us who worry about change.

Beeus Finds Her Way Home

Written by
Sue Spencer Cannon

Her mom was so proud!

where they grazed and played all day.

But one day their human came
to tell them they had
to move.

"What does that mean?" asked Sweetpea.
"Well, you'll all get into my special truck--like this--and ride to your new pasture."

That sounded fine so they all went back to grazing.

All, that is, except for Beeus.
She was worried.
This pasture was the only home she'd ever known.
She didn't want to leave!

"Yoohoo! Eggnog! My mom says we have to leave here.
Have you ever moved?"
"Bock-bock-bock! I've always lived here. Hmmm.
Tough, tough thing my dear lambkin.
What to do-a-roo-a-roo?"

Just then Mr. Nibbles scurried by.
"Hey Mr. Nibbles!
What do you think about moving?"
"Oh, we move every year, Beeus!
You could call me a moving expert.
I think it's fun!"

But that didn't sound fun to Beeus. Sigh.

Mr. Jay was in the tree singing.
"Why so sad, Beeus?"
"My family thinks leaving here is fine."
"Well tweetle-lee-dee! What do you think?"
"I wanna stay here."
"I know what you mean, Beeus! I've always lived around here."

Then Mr. Jay flew away.

That night, snuggling next to her mom, Beeus wondered what she could do to stay in the pasture she loved.
Mr. Jay's never had to move.
And Eggnog will be here...
So secretly she came up with a plan. She was going to stay.

On Moving Day everyone loaded into the truck.
Everyone, that is, except for Beeus.
They all called to her, but she just wouldn't come.
So, they had to leave without her.

As the truck pulled away, they all said a long "Baaaah-bye!"

That night Beeus slept all alone under her favorite oak tree.
No mom. No cousins.
Mr. Nibbles didn't even stop by to see if she was scared--which she was!
She tried to cuddle with the oak tree to get warm but it wasn't very warm or soft.

In the morning Beeus decided she didn't ever want to do that again!
She realized that being Home wasn't being next to a tree, not even your favorite tree!
It was being next to the ones you love!

When her human came to check on her, Beeus ran right up to her. "Oh please! Take me where you took my mom!"

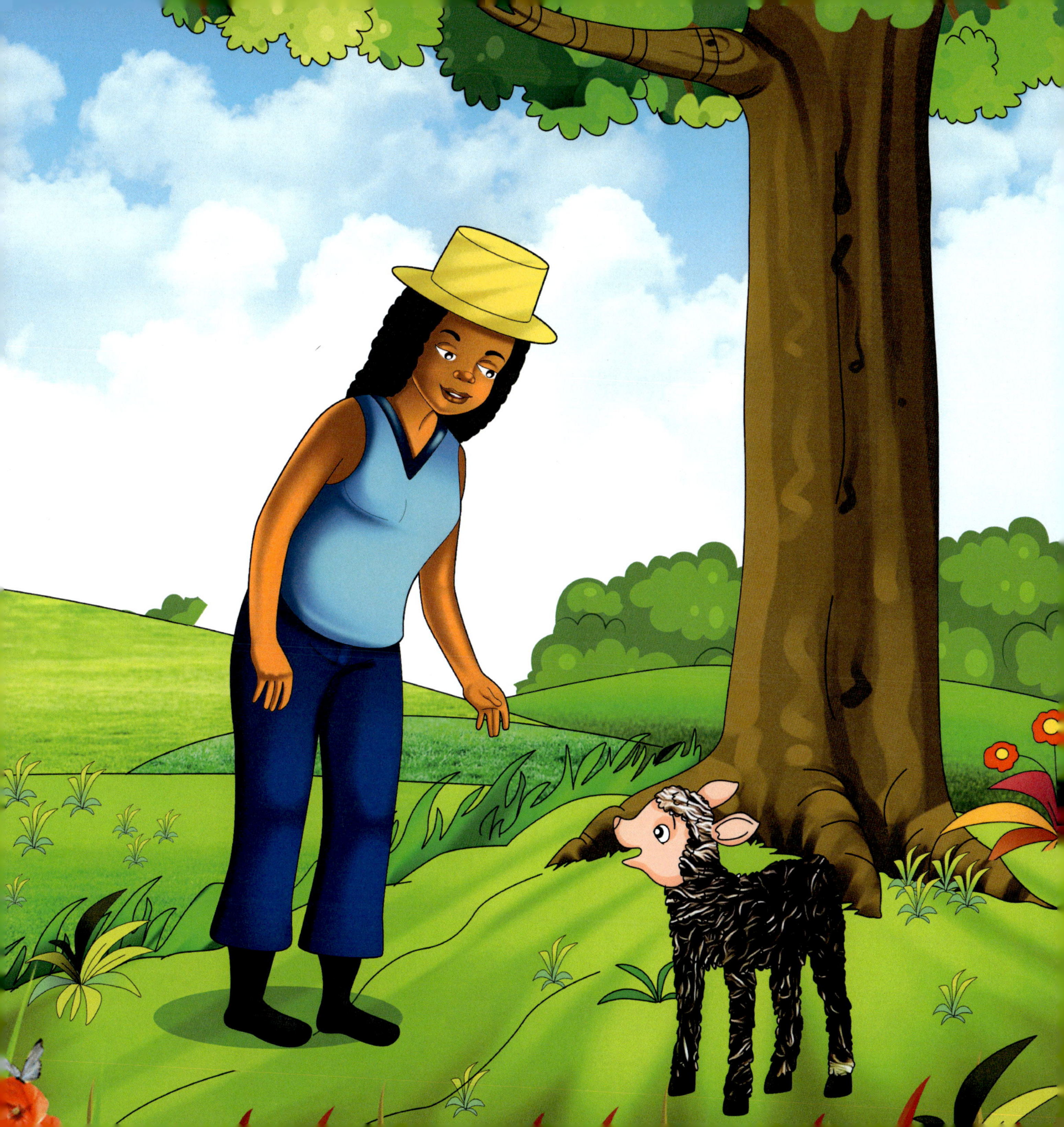

"I'm so sorry. I don't have the special truck.
But I guess I could take you in my Prius."

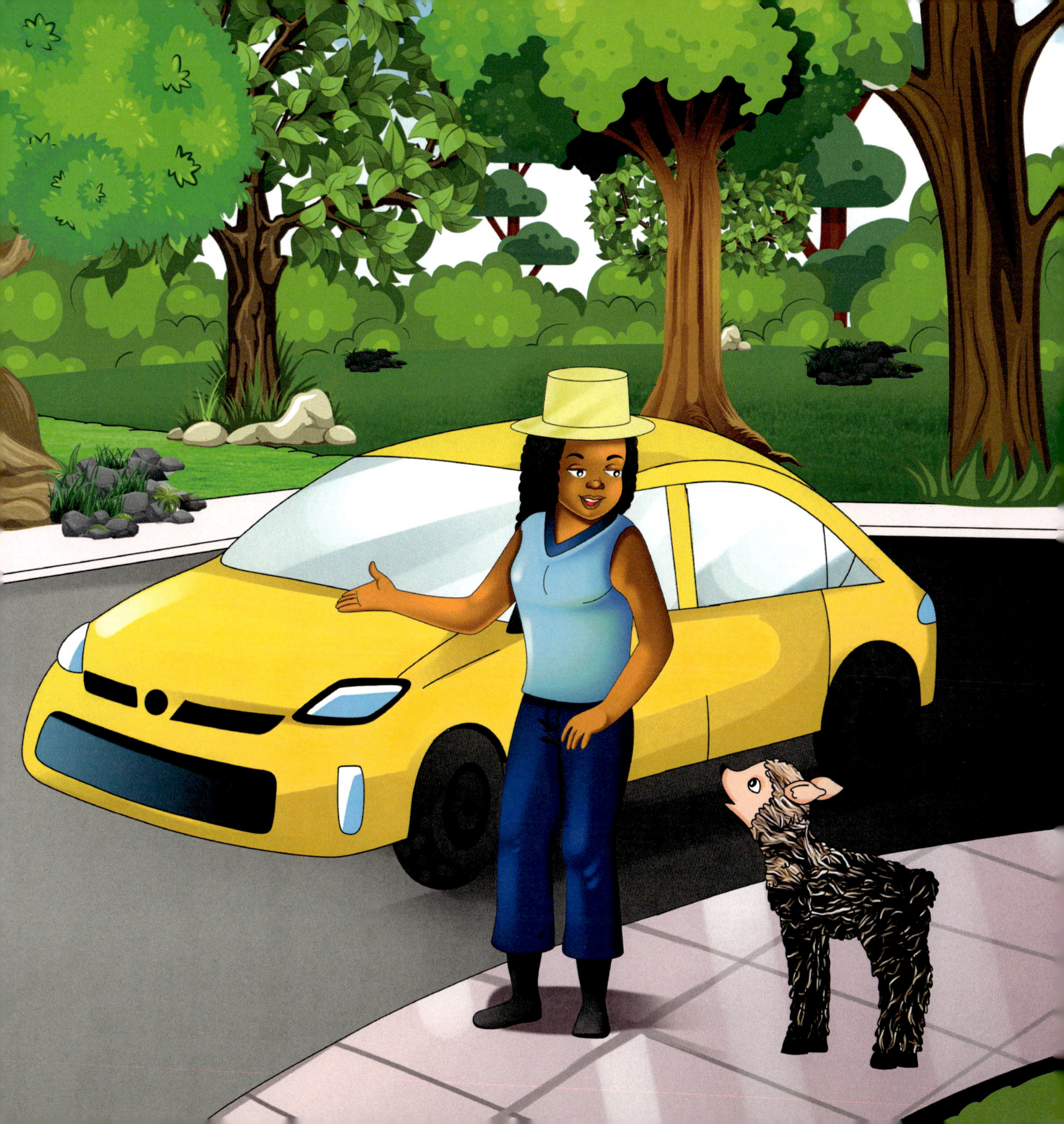

So Beeus climbed into the Prius.

And her human took her Home.

Everyone was relieved to see that Beeus was OK.
They all gave her love snuggles and listened as she told them about her night.

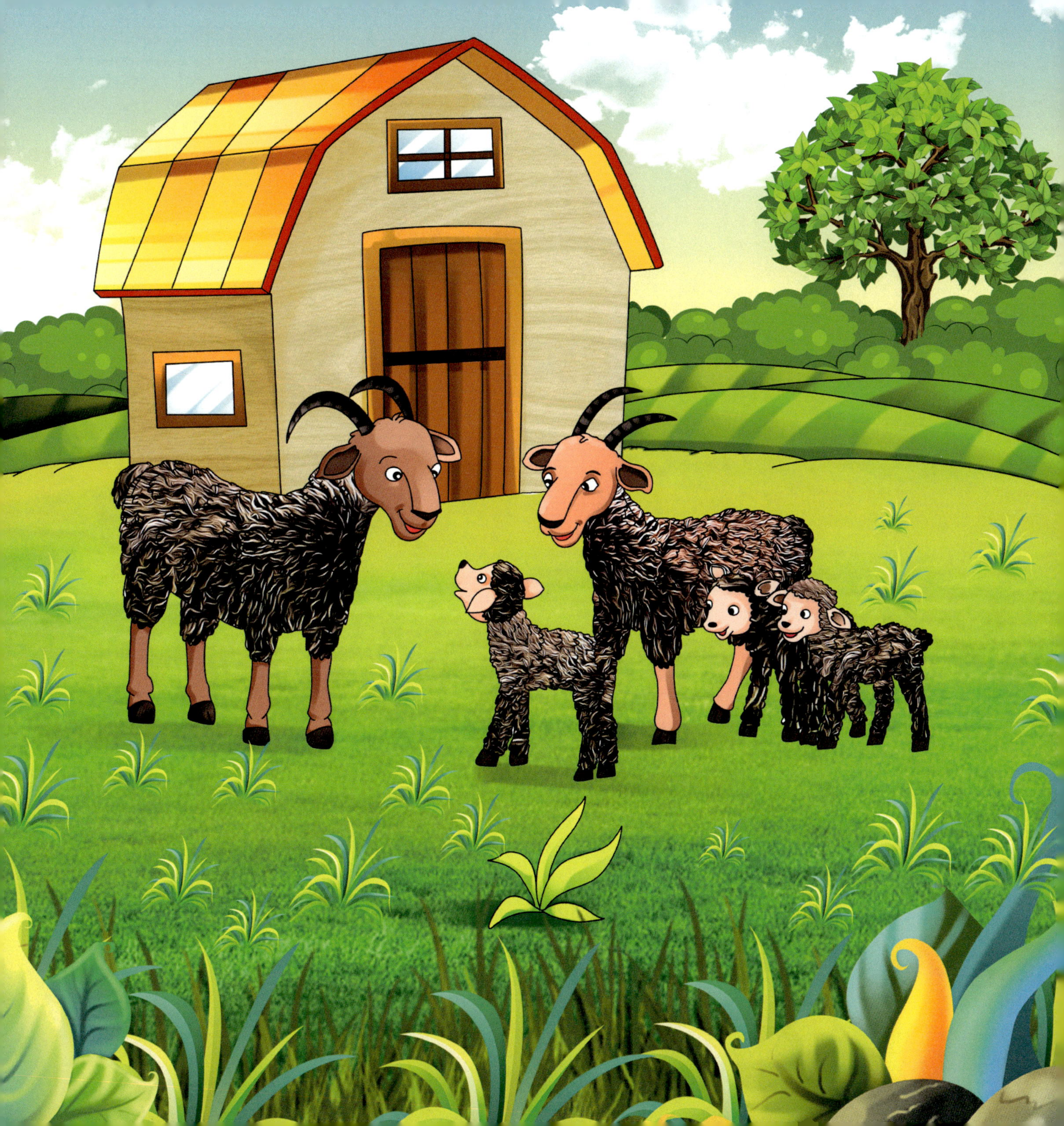

Yes! Beeus was truly Home!

About Beeus

Beeus is a Soay sheep. Soays are a type of sheep (a breed) that originally came from the Isle of Kilda off the northwest coast of Scotland. When they are full-grown, the ewes (females) weigh about 55 pounds and the rams (males) weigh about 75 pounds. They are very hardy sheep. The ewes are very good mothers and their lambs like Beeus are as cute as can be. Their wooly coats don't need to be trimmed (sheared) each year like most sheep because they shed their coats each spring. You can learn more about Soays and other breeds of sheep by checking out these websites:
https://en.wikipedia.org/wiki/Soay_sheep
https://saltmarshranch.com/about-soay/small-sheep-small-acreage.shtml
https://soaysheep.bio.ed.ac.uk/meet-sheep

About the Author

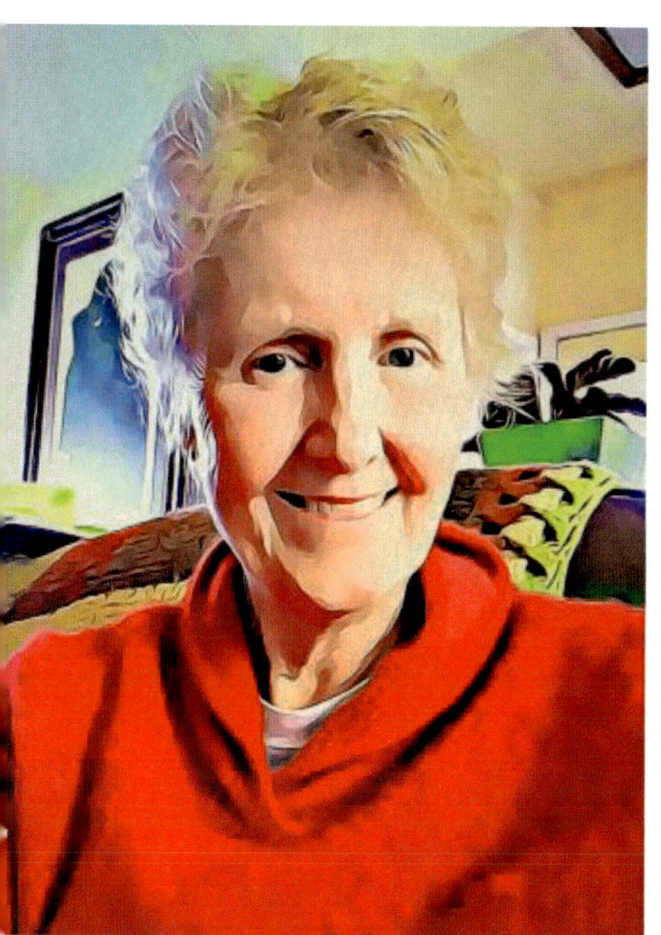

Sue Cannon is a retired amateur rancher. She spent over 10 years living on a ranch in the beautiful rolling hills of the San Francisco North Bay Area. During that time she cared for a small flock of Soay sheep. Each spring they had several young lambs that went to new homes when they were 2 or 3 months old.

When Sue retired she found a loving new home for her sheep. And just like in the story, one stayed behind, unwilling to leave her lovely pasture home. Beeus' story is based on this.

Sue is also a retired Registered Nurse. She worked in Adult ICUs for over 20 years. Her previous writings include poems and a dissertation about a 12th-Century nun named Hildegard of Bingen.

https://books.google.com/books/about/
The_Medicine_of_Hildegard_of_Bingen.html?id=psUfAQAAMAAJ

Made in United States
Orlando, FL
02 March 2023